PREHISTORY

Mike Corbishley
Tim Darvill
Peter Stone

ENGLISH HERITAGE

CONTENTS

CLOCKWISE FROM TOP: Boxgrove man, palaeolithic handaxe, Silbury Hill, Grimes Graves, Stonehenge.

About this book

As a species, we seem fascinated by our past and appear eager to understand more about it. This is difficult enough when discussing something that happened years, decades, or centuries ago. If an event happened recently, there may be people who lived through it who can help explain what went on. But in the case of recent events, everyone will probably have a slightly different understanding of what actually happened. Sometimes, those who were there deliberately mis-interpret what happened for their own benefit: there is much truth in the saying that 'history is written by the winners'.

When there is no-one still alive to help explain what happened, we have to rely on things people wrote down - accounts which are often biased as they are written from a particular viewpoint. Frequently, such written explanations can be elaborated, checked, confirmed or shown to be false by carefully studying the physical evidence left by events. For example, we can visit the trenches left by the opposing armies during the First World War, see the appalling conditions in which prisoners have been kept at various times in the past, or chart the rise in luxury of medieval castles as they turned from places of military security to palaces of imposing grandeur.

However, as we go further back in time our reliance on the written word diminishes as the number of accounts of any particular event become fewer (and are frequently written a long time after the event). As this happens our reliance on the physical evidence of the past increases to the point that it becomes the only evidence for what happened. In other words, when we arrive at a time before writing, at the time we call prehistor, archaeology is our only source.

Prehistory is not a short, irrelevant period of the past where nothing happened, with the human population waiting for civilisation to arrive in the form of Roman legions. Quite the contrary chronologically, it accounts for over 99% of the human past. During this time our earliest human ancestors spread across the world from

ABOVE: **Prehistoric music and storytelling event for schools at Maiden Castle, Dorset.**
LEFT: **Pupils at the Alexander Keiller Museum at Avebury, Wiltshire.**
BELOW: **Pupils on a visit to Hetty Peglar's Tump long barrow in Gloucestershire.**

Africa and changed, modified and evolved until our own species, *Homo sapiens sapiens*, made its appearance some 200,000 years ago. It was during prehistory that all of the important pre-industrial discoveries and inventions that define the human race were made including the development of speech, the modification of natural objects into tools, the use and control of fire, and the domestication of plants for food and animals for food and labour.

The events of prehistory make us what we are as a species today and bond us together in a way that no events of history can do. Some study of prehistory is therefore essential to any broad and balanced curriculum as it provides an understanding of our common past and achievements. In particular, introducing pupils to prehistory will help emphasise the multi-cultural dimensions of our collective past.

This book provides an outline of the prehistory of the British Isles and suggests a number of ways in which the study of prehistory can be fitted into school curricula: not as a forced added extra but as an integral, relevant and exciting component where pupils are encouraged to think and learn in a structured and logical way that will serve them well for the rest of their lives.

TIMELINE

An artist's impression of the landscape at Boxgrove 500.000 years ago (see page 6).

500,000 BC
Land bridge between what is now Britain and the Continent.
Homo erectus hunters present

225,000
Neanderthal people
(*Homo neanderthalensis*) in Britain

40,000
Modern humans (*Homo sapiens sapiens*) arrive in Britain and elsewhere in Europe

30,000
First cave art in Europe

12-10,000
Last ice sheets retreat, woodland develops

7,000
First farmers in the Balkans, Greece and southern Italy

5,000
Farmers in central and western Europe

4,000
Horses domesticated in eastern Europe

4500-3000
Farming begins in Britain, settlements and burial monuments.
Hunting still practised

3000
Circular 'ritual' monuments constructed, including henges.
Round barrows for burial

Objects from Bush Barrow, Wiltshire (see page 14).

Stonehenge (see page 13).

Artist's impression of Star Carr (see page 9).

An artist's impression of the building of the final phase of Stonehenge.

2500
Gold, copper and bronze objects first manufactured

2000
First palaces on the island of Crete

1700-1000
Intensive settlement throughout Britain

1050
Widespread use of iron in Greece

1000
Some upland areas abandoned as climate becomes wetter and cooler. Hill-top settlements - hillforts. Round barrows no longer built

776
First Olympic games

An aerial view of the filled-in mine shafts at Grimes Graves, Norfolk (see page 11).

700
Wheeled vehicles first used

400
Many hillforts out of use

100
Complex 'Celtic' society. More than 1 million people living in Britain

A gold coin of Cunobelin, king of the Trinovantes (see page 20).

59-61
Julius Caesar conquers Gaul

55 & 54
Caesar invades Britain

AD 43
Roman Emperor Claudius invades Britain. Roman conquest begins

The main entrance and earthwork defences of Maiden Castle hillfort, Dorset (see page 19).

In this book dates in prehistory are followed by the letters 'BC' meaning 'Before Christ'. Dates are counted backwards - so the smallest dates are the most recent. 'AD' is an abbreviated form of 'Anno Domini' meaning 'In the year of the Lord' and is put before the date.

Some books about prehistory use the letters 'BP' meaning 'Before Present Time' as the short period of time since the birth of Christ is meaningless for periods hundreds of thousands of years ago. The abbreviation 'BCE' is also sometimes used meaning 'Before the Common Era' and is the same, in date terms, as 'BC'.

You will still find the names for prehistoric periods based on the 'Three Age System' of stone, bronze and iron. They are

Palaeolithic (before 10,000BC)
Old Stone Age of early hunters.

Mesolithic
(10,000BC to 4,400BC)
Middle Stone Age hunters and food gatherers after the last ice age.

Neolithic
(4,400BC to 2,500BC)
New Stone Age farmers.

Bronze Age
(2,500BC to 800 BC)

Iron Age
(800BC to Roman invasion)

The names for the stone ages are taken from Greek words. Palaeo- (old), Meso- (middle), Neo- (new) and -lithic from lithos meaning stone.

An artist's impression of a Bronze Age house based on excavations at Brean Down, Somerset.

IN AMONGST THE ICE

THE FIRST EUROPEANS

We do not know when people first visited or settled in what is now Britain but it was almost certainly when they would have been able to walk over dry land in what is now the English Channel. Best estimates currently suggest it was around half a million years ago, at a time when much of the northern hemisphere was gradually being colonized by a hominid species known as *Homo erectus*.

Glaciations and settlements

Finding out about these people is difficult because during this period the whole of northern Europe underwent a series of glaciations punctuated by warmer periods when people could live in the area.

During cold periods ice-sheets and glaciers would have covered much of northern Britain, and on occasions would have pushed south to what is now the English Channel. Each new glaciation destroyed most of the remains left by previous groups of people. Ahead of the glaciers there was always a region of barren tundra, similar to landscapes today in northern Canada and Siberia. Early human communities whose lifestyles were adapted to cold climates, could live on the tundra (partly frozen landscape with little vegetation) and hunt on the ice-flows as the Nunamiut of Alaska do today.

In warm periods, with the ice-caps as far to the north as they are today, climatic conditions allowed animals to roam freely across massive areas of modern Europe from the Pennines to the Urals in the east and the Alps to the south. At times there were grass plains, but for some periods this north European plain was more or less wooded. Communities who were used to these different environments, moved about pursuing herds of wild horse, deer, bison, wild cattle, elephant, rhinoceros and hippopotamus.

A hunter's camp at Boxgrove

An artist's impression of the landscape at Boxgrove 500,000 years ago.

A hunters'camp at Boxgrove
The oldest site in Britain for which we have a date is Boxgrove near Chichester in West Sussex. Here, by a fluke of preservation, it has been possible to excavate a land surface occupied about 500,000 years ago. Scattered over this landscape are the remains left by groups of hunters who came to collect fresh flint from an eroding cliff and to hunt animals. A fragment of human leg bone (tibia) and two human teeth (not necessarily from the same person) are the remains of the earliest European yet known. Scientific work on the tibia suggests that it came from an adult male who stood about 1.8m tall, weighed about 80kg, and, from the muscle attachments on the bone, was probably a good runner.

These people may have occupied caves but, more probably, lived in small tented encampments, although no such evidence has yet been found. Most evidence recovered so far is of small scatters of flint working debris, each representing the place where somebody sat down and produced a few tools or weapons. The tools, which include handaxes, were used to kill and cut-up animals. At one point a wild horse had been butchered and the best pieces of meat taken away. The remains of beaver, wolf, bear, mink, badger, giant deer, roe deer and aurochs (wild cattle, now extinct) were also found, some at least being the result of successful hunting or scavenging. There is also evidence of fire.

Boxgrove was probably an area that people returned to time and again. It was sheltered and the cliffs would have made it easy to recognize. More importantly, it was an area potentially rich in sources of food. To the north was an upland, at the foot of the cliff a flat grassy plain, and to the south was the sea.

The extent of the ice around 700,000BC.

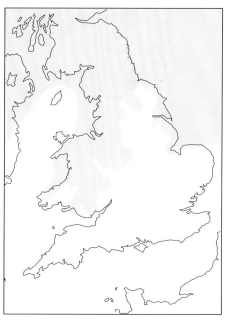

The extent of the ice from around 120,000 to 10,000BC.

Britain before 8,000BC. The broken line indicates sea while Britain is still part of the continent (see page 8).

There is some debate as to whether early humans were scavengers living off the remains of animals killed by other beasts, or whether they were hunters in their own right. In fact, both means of survival probably played a part, supplemented by fishing and collecting edible plants, fruits and tubers. Many communities were mobile, some perhaps migrating long distances, crossing a series of different environments during the course of a year or more. Other groups were more specialized: reindeer hunters following the herds which provided their means of survival, or fishing communities which were able to feed off the seasonal abundance of different species on the coast or in rivers and inland lakes.

THE NEANDERTHALS

By about 225,000 BC, however, the human population and the kinds of tools they used had changed. *Homo erectus* was succeeded by another early human species *Homo neanderthalensis*. Like previous peoples, the Neanderthals sometimes lived in caves. But, more commonly, they used temporary encampments beside rivers or lakes, as at Baker's Hole, Northfleet, Kent.

Neanderthal skeletal remains are known from two sites in the British Isles: Pontnewydd Cave in Clwyd, Wales, and La Cotte de Saint-Brelade on Jersey in the Channel Islands.

MODERN PEOPLE

Modern humans, *Homo sapiens sapiens*, arrived in northern Europe about 40,000 BC and made new styles of flint and stone tools. A great deal of research has gone into the possible relationships between modern humans and earlier peoples. Two theories have been suggested:

■ the first is known as the 'out of Africa' theory in which modern humans developed in the equatorial

Palaeolithic handaxe from the river gravels at Bemerton, Salisbury. Handaxes are so-called because they were thought to be hand-held and used as a general purpose tool for chopping and cutting.

zone and spread into other parts of the world replacing existing populations

■ the alternative theory is the 'multi-regional' one in which there was only one early major dispersal of hominid populations (*Homo erectus*) from Africa followed by broadly parallel evolution in different parts of the world to produce today's, slightly different, modern populations.

THE LAST ICE AGE

In this last ice age, ice-sheets at their most extensive extended as far south as a line between Milford Haven and Flamborough Head. Many of the people formerly living in Britain gradually moved south, occupying parts of central and southern France and Spain. But some remained, joined by hunters from further north and east for whom life in a cold environment was already second nature. Nothing remains of their activity on the ice-flows, but just off the ice-covered lands there is archaeological evidence for the existence of these groups, for example a burial, from the Gower peninsula of south Wales, known as the Red Lady of Paviland (actually a man who was wrongly identified when excavated in 1823) covered in red ochre and buried in a cave. The bones have been dated to about 16,500 BC.

RECOLONIZING THE NORTH

The last ice sheets retreated from Britain between 12,000 and 10,000 BC. Extensive ice sheets still existed further north, however, locking up vast amounts of water which thawed only gradually. The sea level in northern Europe therefore was low, and the British Isles were attached to Europe. The English Channel and the North Sea were dry land, crossed by a few rivers and interrupted at intervals by large lakes formed in hollows scooped out by earlier ice-flows. As the climate warmed, many species of plants and animals gradually recolonized the land as it slowly developed from barren tundra into woodland dominated by pine and birch. Human groups prospered too, and their return to the British Isles marks the beginning of a continuous occupation of the area down to the present day.

New hunting grounds

The extensive new hunting grounds created by the retreat of the ice sheets appear to have been heavily exploited by communities using flint and bone tools and weapons similar to those used over very wide areas of northern Europe at this time. There is evidence of regional variations however, and, within the British Isles, there were probably a series of territories occupied by similar, yet distinct, groups. Among the distinctive tools and weapons found at sites such as Creswell Crags in Derbyshire and Star Carr in North Yorkshire are large leaf-shaped flint points and barbed harpoons made of bone. Small but finely worked flint blades known as *microliths* were probably the barbs of spears and harpoons with wooden shafts.

Like previous peoples, the inhabitants used caves as shelters where they were available. Their links with other European groups is demonstrated by the fact that some pieces of bone have been found decorated with neatly incised pictures of animals. They are in a style similar to those on the walls of painted caves in southern France and northern Spain where such

work coincides with the period when the British Isles were mainly covered by ice sheets.

By about 10,000 BC the transformation from open tundra to woodland inhabited by animals such as red and roe deer, wild boar and cattle was complete. The climate was warmer, and deep rich soils developed.

Microliths from Wiltshire set in a modern reconstruction of a barbed arrowhead.

BRITAIN BECOMES AN ISLAND

Between about 8000 BC and 6000 BC rising sea-levels severed the land-bridge between Britain and the continent. From this time people in Britain appear to have developed their own lifestyles, similar yet slightly different, to those in continental Europe. This was also a time when the native woodland underwent further changes, beginning to

cover most of the country in a relatively dense oak, elm and birch forest.

The increase in forest and the loss of significant areas of land to the sea significantly reduced the land available for settlement and hunting. This in turn suggests there were higher populations in those areas still easily available for settlement.

NOMADIC BANDS SETTLING DOWN

The picture of life about 5000 BC is one of a large number of, but widely scattered, communities dependent mostly on red deer, wild cattle, wild boar, plants, and, on the coastal marine resources. There may have been quite a lot of seasonal movement between a base-camp and temporary hunting camps although the distances covered by any one group probably became less as time went on. Few groups would have lived in the heart of the forests and most seem to have settled around the edges, living as they had before beside rivers, lakes, or coasts. Some groups seem to have cleared small areas of the forest by burning it. This had the effects of:

■ creating artificial areas as suitable places for settlement

■ enhancing the attraction of the area for herds of wild animals who preferred the succulent new shoots of re-growth to the tough fodder of old forest

■ making hunting easier by concentrating the quarry and allowing them to be seen in open ground.

In other ways, life became more complicated. With less mobility, opportunities to collect suitable raw material for making tools and weapons decreased. As a result, small-scale trading links must have developed to move both finished items and raw materials to areas devoid of flint or good stone.

A summer camp at Star Carr

In about 7500 BC the Vale of Pickering was a shallow lake in a fairly well-wooded countryside with birch, pine, willow and hazel. Around the lake there was open countryside with a grass and sedge cover. Here, next to the lake, was a small seasonal settlement. Because the site was waterlogged and peat formed after the site was abandoned, many organic materials such as bone and wood have been preserved that usually do not survive.

The settlement had been built on a brushwood platform, perhaps with a narrow landing stage made from felled birch trees providing access to the lake. A wooden paddle shows that the occupants of the site used boats or canoes. Hunting provided the main source of food and over half of the animals killed were young deer. However, more important for the diet were the wild cattle. Each of these animals provided nearly five times as much meat as a young deer. They also hunted elk, wild pig, pine martens, red fox, and beavers. Bones of a domesticated dog, the earliest yet known in Britain, were found. Surprisingly, there were no fish bones at the site, although they may not have been preserved in the soil conditions at Star Carr.

A wide range of weapons and tools were found including:

■ *microliths* (small worked flints) that would have been part of hunting weapons

■ barbed harpoon tips, made from bone and antler, probably used for fishing

■ flint adzes and axes used for felling trees and making the wooden platform on which the settlement was built.

A bone mattock head suggests that roots and tubers were also collected from the adjacent dryland, although no direct evidence has survived.

The site appears to have been used for making and repairing tools and weapons, and for processing animal skins to make leather clothes. A collection of 21 frontlets from deer skulls, the antlers still attached, have been interpreted as some kind of headdress either for ceremonial purposes or to disguise hunters stalking animals in open woodland. Stone pendants and haematite beads provide a glimpse of the range of personal ornaments worn.

Star Carr was occupied mainly during the summer, perhaps with occasional visits during the spring and autumn. It was a temporary hunting camp with the main camp probably on higher ground.

An artist's impression of Star Carr.

SOCIAL CHANGE

One of the biggest social revolutions in history took place, in Britain, between 4500 and 3000 BC. Attitudes to the world seem to have changed markedly, and with this changed much of the way of life. It was probably not a rapid change, but a very gradual process. Collectively, the changes mark the beginning of what archaeologists have called the Neolithic period.

One of the most visible indications of this change is farming which originated in the Near East and spread northwards and westwards across Europe. Whether it was adopted in Britain as a result of colonization by farming communities or by native hunter-gatherer groups learning farming techniques from farmers on the continent is impossible to say, although the most likely explanation involves a little of both. Certainly, for a time hunter-gatherers existed alongside early farmers and may have competed for land and resources.

THE CHANGING LANDSCAPE

Early farming communities had a considerable impact on the landscape, most notably by clearing woodland, introducing cereals (wheat and barley), and establishing grassland pasture for cattle, pigs, and sheep. Not all areas were settled by these early farmers. Well drained, easily cultivated land attracted most interest, especially major river valleys and downlands of central and southern England.

New settlements

Settlements became more permanent and more substantial. Farmsteads with perhaps one or two rectangular wooden houses were dotted about the countryside. Around each would have been a few small fields or gardens carved out of the surrounding woodland.

Throughout southern and eastern England a series of large ditched enclosures, called by archaeologists causewayed enclosures, were built. A few, such as Crickley Hill, Gloucestershire, and Carn Brae in Cornwall, seem to have been defended settlements or small villages. Others, like Windmill Hill,

The long barrow at West Kennet, Wiltshire is 100m long.

Wiltshire, appear to have been seasonal meeting places where communities could gather together for ceremonies, to exchange raw materials and things they had made, and to meet old friends and potential marriage partners.

Ceremony and ritual

All of these enclosures combined domestic activities with ceremony and ritual. In the minds of these early farmers everyday life and the supernatural appear to have been inextricably linked. For the first time distinct structures to bury their dead were built. At first, burial monuments were small structures, usually of stone, although where no stone was available, timber and earth were used instead.

THE AGE OF THE LONG BARROWS

After about 3500 BC the tradition of building small, simple tombs was replaced by the development of very much larger monuments - long barrows. These massive structures may be up to 100m long and must have taken an enormous effort to construct.

The burial rites which took place at long barrows appear to have been complicated and lengthy involving not only funerals but also ceremonies at which bones from partly decomposed corpses were moved about within the different sections of the barrow. Long barrows also appear to have been more than just burial monuments. Their great size and the fact that only small parts of them were used for burials suggests they had other uses too. Set away from settlements, often on a prominent hill, these monuments were probably used to mark the territory of the community who built and used them.

Occasionally, highly visible rocks seem to have been singled out for special attention, as with some of the natural tors on Bodmin Moor. Elsewhere, large blocks of stone were set upright as standing stones, beginning a tradition that carried on for thousands of years. Simple designs, cup-marks and rings were chipped into some natural rock outcrops and boulders. Rivers and wet places began to attract attention too, and numerous stone axes from this period have been found in rivers as if deliberately thrown there for ritual purposes.

NEW INVENTIONS

Among the other changes associated with the development of farming was the introduction of pottery, and the manufacture of a wide range of new tools and weapons. Some of these are very fine and show a high level of skill in their design and manufacture.

Obtaining good stone for making tools posed something of a problem. Surface outcrops were used wherever they were suitable, but many of these, as at Great Langdale in Cumbria, were difficult to reach and the best raw materials sometimes lay underground. Mines for flint were established all across the chalk lands of southern England, for example at Cissbury in Sussex, and Grimes Graves in Norfolk. These were massive undertakings, an individual shaft perhaps taking 12 people two months to dig. At Cissbury there are upwards of 100 known shafts.

TRADE AND COMMUNICATIONS

The exchange networks developed during earlier periods to allow the movement of raw material and finished items between

Flint mining at Grimes Graves

From about 2100 BC, the farmers living around Grimes Graves, near Thetford in Norfolk, began to dig open pits to mine the seams of flint below the surface. They dug over 700 pits, some about 10 metres deep, to reach the best seam of flint. From the open pits, the miners dug horizontal shafts to follow the seam. The chalk and waste flint was tipped into the nearest worked-out pit. Each pit probably produced about eight tonnes of flint.

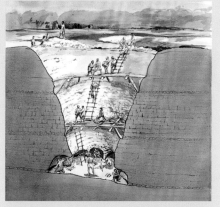

An artist's impression of Grimes Graves.

Working these mines must have been very hard. The miners used only their hands, shovels made from the shoulder blades of oxen and flint tools to shift the sandy soil on the surface. To dig out the chalk and flint, they made picks from the antlers cast off red deer and wedges of bone and flint hammer stones.

The flint they mined was made into all sorts of tools, such as axes, arrow and spearheads, knives and scrapers for cleaning the skins of animals. These expert miners probably did not work at Grimes Graves all the time but were farmers as well. The mines continued in use until about 1600 BC.

Grimes Graves was only discovered in the 1870s but the area had been named by the Anglo-Saxons from the words 'graves' meaning hollows and 'grim' meaning fierce. Grim was also another name for the god Woden. Prehistoric sites were often thought to have been constructed or associated with gods or giants.

Modern props support the shafts at Grimes Graves. At the base of the mine here you can see the large nodules of high quality black flint.

regions continued to develop and expand. In some cases this may have involved people travelling to established sources to get the stone they needed. Material was probably passed from group to group at seasonal gatherings, travelling great distances in a number of small journeys. In this way, flint, stone, pottery, and probably other materials, were moved about between communities. The countryside of Britain must have been criss-crossed by a network of paths and tracks. These would mostly have been little more than the kind of footpaths we are familiar with today. In wet areas, however, something more was needed and in the Somerset Levels, for example, timber trackways were built so that people could cross the wetlands in safety.

Not everything that was traded was for everyday use. Luxury items were moved about too, including very fine polished stone axes meant for show, not for use. The finest of

all were jadeite axes made in northern Italy or Switzerland which found their way into all parts of the British Isles, suggesting a society also used to long distance trading by sea.

Evidence for conflict. A leaf-shaped flint arrowhead was found in the chest cavity of a skeleton lying at the bottom of the ditch which surrounded the enclosure at Hambledon Hill, Dorset.

CONFLICT AND CONTESTED LAND

One of the most numerous kind of flint artefact known from the period are leaf-shaped arrowheads. Some may have been used for hunting wild animals, and certainly hunting made an important contribution to the diet of these communities. But shooting at each other seems to have been equally common, and a small proportion of adults buried in long barrows appear to have been killed by arrow-shot. At some causewayed enclosures, notably Crickley Hill, Gloucestershire, and Hambledon Hill, Dorset, there is evidence for large-scale attacks that led to the destruction of the settlements.

Whether this fighting was between farmers and hunter-gatherers, or between neighbouring groups of farmers is not clear. It has been suggested, however, that the issues being fought over were simple ones - rights to land or resources.

THE AGE OF STONEHENGE

Around 3000 BC there appears to have been a decline in the population across much of southern England. Long barrows were no longer built and those still in use were deliberately blocked up. Causewayed enclosures were abandoned. Woodland grew back on land which had been cleared. In the far west and north of Britain change was less rapid and less marked.

About this time there seems to have been a special concern for constructing extremely long narrow monuments. Examples of a new type of monument, the cursus, were built in many areas. Cursus monuments were long, narrow enclosures bounded by a bank and outer ditch. They are frequently associated with rivers. The Springfield cursus in Essex is 700m long by 40m wide and has been extensively excavated. Near the eastern end were the remains of a timber structure and pits and scoops containing the remains of fires and burnt bone. The purpose of cursus monuments is unclear, but it is assumed they were used for some kind of ceremony which involved processions. Springfield is by no means the largest, the Dorset Cursus is about 10km long.

NEW MONUMENTS AND NEW IDEOLOGIES

The building of large linear monuments around 3000 BC may, however, be the final throws of a dying tradition. Shortly afterwards, in all parts of Britain, there emerged a very clear interest in a range of circular monuments.

Common to many of these structures is an increasing interest in the movements of the sun, especially the mid-summer and mid-winter rising and setting positions. This is not to say, however, that the monuments were built as observatories. The special alignment of these monuments may have had more to do with determining the appropriate timing for particular ceremonies or events.

An aerial view of Avebury, Wiltshire.

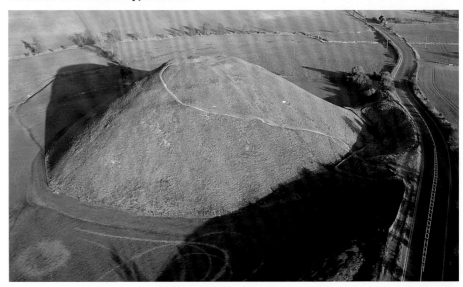

Silbury Hill, Wiltshire is the largest prehistoric constructed mound in Europe.

An artist's impression of the construction of Silbury Hill. The chalk rubble and earth needed for building were excavated from a ditch around the mound, which covers an area of 2.2 ha (5.5 acres) and is 40m high. Its construction would have taken the equivalent of 500 workers toiling every day for 10 years.

THE AGE OF STONEHENGE

Stonehenge

Stonehenge and the landscape in which it stands are unique. Sited within an area of less than two square kilometres are hundreds of prehistoric monuments built between 5,000 and 3,000 years ago. The most famous element of this landscape is the stone circle, which when complete, formed a circle of upright stones topped by lintels of local sandstone, and the smaller 'bluestones' - almost certainly transported especially to the site from south Wales, some 240 miles (385 km) away. But the monument had a complex history, as the artist's impressions and drawings on page 27 show.

Stonehenge today.

Round barrows

Round barrows are the most numerous and widely distributed type of prehistoric burial monument. They began to be built during early Neolithic times, and continue well into the Bronze Age. Most cover inhumations (the burial of whole corpses), although in some parts of the country cremation was preferred. Grave goods are sometimes included with the deceased, sometimes a pot or some personal ornaments such as a belt or a flint knife.

Passage graves

A few regions of the British Isles developed the use of highly distinctive tombs in the later Neolithic. In West Penwith, Cornwall and on the Isles of Scilly a series of small stone-built tombs known as entrance graves were built. Circular in plan, these monuments are rarely over 4m across. The chamber, rectangular in plan, is accessible from the edge of the mound.

In Anglesey, North Wales and in Orkney, Scotland there are particularly impressive groups of burial monuments known as Developed Passage Graves. All the Developed Passage Graves are large, over 10m in diameter, and have a central stone-built chamber approached from the outside of the mound by way of a long passage. The example at Maes Howe, Orkney, is aligned so that the last rays of the setting sun on midwinter's day shine into the chamber.

Perhaps the builders saw a link between the setting sun and death as represented by the burials in the tomb. Some of the stones used in the construction of Developed Passage Graves were decorated with spirals, lozenges and zig-zag lines.

Henges, circles, rows and avenues

The most distinctive structures of the new kinds of late Neolithic circular monuments are henges. These have a substantial ditch, outside of which is a bank. Typically they have one or two entrances, but occasionally as many as four were built, as at the largest known example, Avebury, Wiltshire. Inside some henges archaeologists have found postholes representing the remains of what must have been timber circles or structures. Elsewhere, again as at Avebury, the interior contains one or more stone circles.

Stone circles are also found without accompanying henges. In fact the majority of known examples are set on their own. The earliest stone circles were generally small rings with closely set stones and clearly defined entrances, for example Castlerigg, Cumbria. A little later came large open circles with widely spaced stones such as the Hurlers, Cornwall where there are four such circles in a line. When excavated, many stone circles are found to be replacements of timber circles. Like henges, the stone circles are interpreted as ceremonial meeting places and, since henges and circles sometimes exist together, it is likely that they were used in much the same way.

BELOW: The stone circle at Castlerigg, Cumbria.

INTERNATIONAL LINKS AND THE DEVELOPMENT OF METALWORKING

The period 3000-2000 BC saw an increase in contact with mainland Europe. Goods and ideas were regularly exchanged, and as part of this process the expertise to produce metal objects almost certainly came to Britain from the continent.

Gold and copper were the first metals to be worked, followed shortly afterwards by bronze (an alloy of copper, tin and lead). The introduction of metalworking about 2500 BC traditionally marks the start of the Bronze Age, but the new technology did little for the majority of the population as most of the early products were luxury items such as ceremonial daggers, trinkets, and ornaments. Everyday tools and weapons were still manufactured in flint and stone.

Another product of the increasing international contacts was the arrival in Britain of 'Beaker' pottery. Beaker pottery is distinctive because of its high quality, fine decoration, and beautifully curved shapes. The appearance of beakers was once explained as an invasion by the 'Beaker People', but beakers are now thought to have been introduced as part of more widespread trading and exchange systems.

WARRIORS AND AN ELITE SOCIETY

Many features of late Neolithic society suggest that it was hierarchically organized and that various kinds of specialist were present. Some people seem to be buried on their own with a lot of grave goods while others have nothing at all. While it is dangerous to equate the quantity of grave goods associated with an individual in death with wealth and status in life, some kind of link can be expected, especially given the high quality of the best grave-goods which include metalwork, beautifully made flint work, and pottery.

One of the most distinctive grave goods are items related to warfare, especially archery equipment and daggers that might signify a warrior class.

RIGHT: An artist's impression of the burial at Bush Barrow. Stonehenge can be seen in the background.

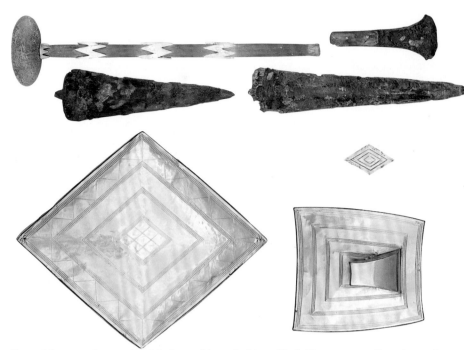

One of the most famous burials from this period is at Bush Barrow, near Stonehenge in Wiltshire. The body of a man was found with a variety of high quality objects including decorated gold ornaments, three daggers, a bronze axe and a stone macehead with bone fittings for the handle (reconstructed here).

The wealth and prestige of the late Neolithic upper class was probably based on its position within long-distance trading networks and the ability of individuals to acquire exotic goods in return for raw materials.

The upper class displayed its power not only through the objects they wore and used, but in the monuments and structures they encouraged, or perhaps coerced, their communities to build. Building cursus monuments, henges and stone circles required an immense amount of labour and co-ordination of effort. It can be argued that only a hierarchical society could achieve this.

By implication, late Neolithic peoples must have operated within relatively restricted geographical areas. This can be glimpsed archaeologically by the fairly regular spacing at intervals of about 40km of major ceremonial centres which variously combine henges, stone circles, enclosures of various sorts, cursus monuments, and groups of round barrows. It is easy to imagine that each of these ceremonial centres was the focal point in the life of a particular community. Whether the local populations lived in fixed permanent villages at this time is not clear.

PEOPLE EVERYWHERE AND A GOOD CLIMATE

The pattern of society established in the later Neolithic continued through into the Bronze Age, becoming more regionalised in its character and more extensive in its use of the landscape. Upland areas such as Dartmoor, the North York Moors, the Pennines and the Cheviots were intensively farmed up to altitudes of over 250m above sea level, while the already occupied lowlands continued in use as well. One interpretation of this is that the population was rising.

One reason behind this expansion was a short-lived change in the climate, with dryer and warmer conditions prevailing. This allowed communities to make use of higher ground, including growing crops well above what would now be regarded as marginal land. These areas have not been used for intensive settlement since the Bronze Age, and the fields and farms created in prehistoric times still survive in remarkably good condition.

An artist's impression of the village buildings at Grimspound, Devon. BELOW: Grimspound today.

RE-ORGANIZING THE LANDSCAPE

The most impressive aspect of the early Bronze Age expansion of settlement was that for the first time, much of the landscape was organized in a regular way. Evidence from preserved, ancient pollen taken from peat bogs and old lakes suggests that a great deal of woodland was cleared. In these areas large regular field systems, paddocks and grazing areas were laid out. From this it is possible to see that the power wielded by the leaders of each group, and the labour they controlled, being switched from the construction of ceremonial sites to the widespread restructuring of the landscape for farming.

Some communities constructed their field systems with houses grouped together among the fields. Others adopted a pattern involving farmsteads or enclosed settlements set apart from or central to their fields and grazing areas. Village-size settlements of anything up to 50 dwellings are known in upland areas of the west of England, for example Grimspound and Rider's Rings on Dartmoor. Smaller groupings representing the settlements of one or two extended families are more common in eastern and southern England, for example at Itford Hill in Sussex.

DEATH AND CEREMONY

Burial rites changed during the course of the Bronze Age, from the burial of complete corpses to cre-mations. Round barrows, made of earth, were used for the majority of burials, and extensive barrow cemeteries developed including new barrow types: bell barrows, disc barrows, saucer barrows, and pond barrows which have a hollowed-out form. In upland areas, cairns (mounds made of stone) rather than barrows are common.

Ceremonial monuments

Some of the ceremonial and ritual monuments of the later Neolithic continue through into the second millennium BC, others such as henges and cursus monuments

15

were abandoned. The most widely distributed ceremonial monument was the stone circle. Some of these late circles include a stone placed on its side. This pattern of change can be seen very clearly at Stonehenge where the earlier enclosure was abandoned and first a simple open circle and later more complicated circles and horseshoe-shaped settings were constructed.

Stone rows also appear during the early Bronze Age, often incorporating a stone circle or cairn. These rows may be short, as at The Devil's Arrows near Boroughbridge, North Yorkshire, with just 4 stones, or very long as at Merrivale, Dartmoor, with over 40 stones.

Many Bronze Age ceremonial monuments continued to be orientated and aligned in a particular way. This varied from one part of the country to another, but the rising and setting of the sun and moon seem to have continued to interest many communities. Water also appears to have been important, and a good proportion of fine metal objects, especially weapons, continued to be deposited in wet places such as rivers and bogs.

METALWORKING AND CRAFTS

Bronze remained the principal metal worked during the second millennium BC, although gold was used for ornaments. Britain was a major producer of metal ores. Copper mines on the Great Orme in North Wales were among the largest in Europe, and there is evidence for early mining in mid Wales and at Alderley Edge in Cheshire. Copper and tin extraction almost certainly took place in Cornwall too, but no physical evidence has, as yet, been found.

Many more tools and weapons were now made in metal and included daggers, swords, axes, chisels, razors, and a vast range of ornaments and trinkets. Smiths seem to have been working at two different levels. Some operated locally making mainly tools and ornaments in locally distinctive styles. Others operated regionally making mainly weapons and very complicated ornaments which often reflected changing continental fashions.

Other crafts

Metalworking was only one of many crafts practised at this time.

Stone rows at Merrivale on Dartmoor.

Metal was used as parts of artefacts involving other materials, for example wood and bone for handles. Leather was widely used, and there is evidence for weaving from the mid-second millennium BC onwards. Craftspeople continued to work in stone, for example, finely polished tools with holes to fit wooden handles, so-called battle-axes, axe-hammers and mace-heads. Some of these may have been symbols of power and authority as much as functional weapons or tools. Stone was also used for making metalworkers' tools such as touch-stones, hammers, and cushions. Almost every community made their own pottery.

TRADE AND THE EUROPEAN COMMUNITY

Between 2000 and 1000 BC links with mainland Europe and Ireland remained strong. The discovery of two shipwrecks just off the English coast is evidence of travel between southern England and France. In both cases the boats in question were taking metalwork across the Channel. Indeed it was probably because of Britain's involvement in the Europe-wide trade in metal ores that strong continental links were maintained.

To what extent people migrated between England and the continent at this time is not known, although all of what can be seen in the archaeological evidence could be explained as trade and copying rather than invasions or major migrations.

ABANDONING THE UPLANDS

The favourable climate which permitted the expansion of settlement into upland areas began to fade around 1000 BC. Wetter and cooler conditions gradually took over. This had three effects:

■ soil quality declined as nutrients were washed away and hard mineral layers built up in the soil

■ crops could no longer be grown so successfully at high altitudes

■ bog began to form and gradually inundate fields and the open areas between them.

Many areas on the high ground and places with especially sensitive soils had to be abandoned. The changes to the soil and the reduction of vegetation cover meant that the natural succession of scrub and woodland did not take hold after abandonment and these areas became moorland and heaths. This was especially marked in what are now Dartmoor, Exmoor, Bodmin Moor, and the Dorset Heaths. Paradoxically, these areas are today regarded as natural and unspoilt countryside while they are actually the products of human over-exploitation and dramatic climatic change in the Bronze Age.

CONFLICT AND THE RISE OF THE HILLFORT

The first few centuries of the first millennium BC were turbulent times. As upland fields and settlements were abandoned people seem to have retreated to lower ground. Even in southern England arable cultivation declined, and there is some evidence for widespread cattle herding. For whatever reason, it appears that the existing population had to be supported on a smaller land area, a situation which inevitably brings about social and economic stress. There were two very visible signs of this pressure - defended settlements and territorial boundaries.

Defended settlements

The first development was to build defended settlements, usually on hilltops or promontories that provided natural defence. Two kinds can be recognized, the majority of them being in areas adjacent to the most populated uplands: eastern Devon, Somerset, all along the Cotswold escarpment, the Welsh Marches, and across the southern Pennines. One type is the hilltop enclosure: large hillforts which could be used to defend fields and paddocks for livestock at times of trouble. A particularly good example is Nottingham Hill, Gloucestershire, where an area of about 48ha is enclosed. Among the finds known from the site is a hoard of swords, tools and weapons buried in a wooden box perhaps during a period of local unrest.

A second, more widespread, type is represented by small heavily defended settlements. Crickley Hill, Gloucestershire, is a thoroughly excavated example, constructed about 700 BC with a massive timber-laced stone rampart set around an area of 3.8ha which contained six or more long houses and storage facilities for grain.

Territorial boundaries

The second development was the increasing use of linear boundaries to partition the landscape into defined blocks of, presumably, the territories of individual communities. Some of these boundaries are very impressive, massive banks and ditches running for many kilometres across the countryside. Some cut across earlier field systems, others neatly skirt existing fields as if containing them in the newly identified territory.

TECHNOLOGY AND THE FIRST ARMS RACE

The high technological skills of the people of the latter part of the second millennium BC continued into the first millennium, supplemented by new types of tools, weapons and ornaments. As in earlier centuries, contacts with continental Europe provided the inspiration for many of these.

Most notable are developments and changes in weapon technology. Shields and body armour appear first. Swords become more common and in two main types: a thrusting sword for use in hand-to-hand combat, and a slashing sword for use by warriors on horse-back. This is the first time that horses appear to have been used in warfare, and soon after, from around 700 BC, wheeled vehicles appear too. Initially they are very simple carts or wagons, and since there were no roads they must have been of little use except for ceremonial parades on flat ground. Indeed, many of the finest weapons of the late Bronze Age and early Iron Age would have been of little use in battle and must be regarded as ceremonial. However, battles did occur and human skeletons with bronze weapons still embedded in them have been found.

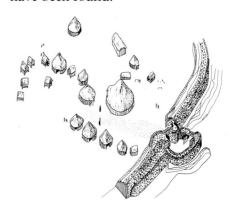

An artist's impression of part of the settlement at Crickley Hill, showing round houses and heavily defended entrance dated to around 500BC.

An aerial view of Crickley Hill, Gloucestershire.

Iron is introduced

From about 700 BC iron began to be worked. Iron had the advantage that it was widely available in areas of Britain where other metals were scarce (for example in south east England) and only required raw material from a single source. Early iron products were simply copies of bronze implements like sickles and razors, but it was not long before iron-smiths got the feel of the new material and developed edged tools which were probably technically superior to bronze tools.

SETTLEMENTS AND FARMS

Outside the main zones of the early hillforts there were all sorts of settlements. Many sites were enclosed, and some show signs that their occupants replaced simple fences with increasingly robust boundary works. This is especially marked in northern England, where a tradition of strongly-fenced enclosures containing perhaps two or three buildings is widespread from Yorkshire and Humberside up to the Scottish borders.

CHANGING BURIAL AND RITUAL

After about 1000 BC people stopped building round barrows and for the next few centuries burials were deposited in flat cemeteries or inserted into the top of existing barrows. Most were cremations, and large pots were often used to contain the ashes of the deceased. By about 700 BC, however, traditional burials were rare. New methods of disposing of the dead which leave little or no archaeological trace must have been used.

Wet places such as bogs, rivers and lakes were popular throughout prehistory, but from about 1000 BC onwards they seem to have become very important focal points. Indeed, they may well have been used for the disposal of the dead. Much of the very finest metalwork made at this time appears to have been deliberately deposited in rivers, lakes and bogs perhaps as grave goods or as dedications to water gods.

The problems of the Celts

Earlier theories about the development of hillforts and new weapons in Britain in the early first millennium BC were linked to migrations or invasions of new people from mainland Europe. Amongst the latest of these migrating groups were peoples sometimes called the Celts. These people, it was believed, were responsible for spreading an art style, the so-called *La Tène* style, and a distinctive Indo-European language which has come down to us as Welsh, Breton, Cornish and Gaelic.

This traditional idea of the Celts can now be seen to be at odds with the archaeological evidence. The development of hillforts and new weapons took place over a long period and appears to have been the result of local traditions with influence from overseas rather than new people. Also, these changes happened two centuries before *La Tène* art-styles became widespread. Finally, the link with the spread of new languages must be discounted too because it is now recognized that Indo-European languages were established much earlier than previously thought, perhaps as far back as the fourth millennium BC.

It is now recognized that there were no such people as 'The Celts' who spread out across Europe. Rather there are a series of related tribal groups who, by about 500 BC, shared a common art-style, met and traded with one another. Groups close by may also have been linked through alliances or kinship. Collectively, these individual and dispersed groups can be referred to as Celts.

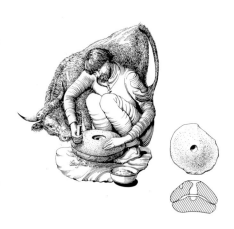

Grinding corn with a two-part rotary quern.

Grinding corn for flour on a saddle-shaped stone quern.

Spinning woollen thread with spindle weighted with a perforated stone.

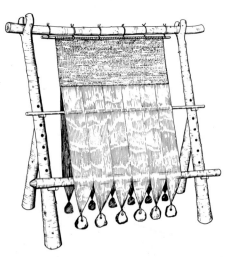

An upright loom for weaving cloth. The vertical warp threads are kept taut with clay weights.

Maiden Castle

The largest Iron Age hillfort in Europe, and the best known in Britain, is Maiden Castle, near Dorchester, Dorset. More than 5,000 years ago early Neolithic farmers marked out a causewayed enclosure on top of this natural hill. Apart from being a place for the occasional burial, the site was deserted until around 500 BC. Iron Age people enclosed the hilltop with deep ditches and high ramparts. The hillfort was doubled in size two hundred years later. The inhabitants added more lines of defence especially at the main entrance until there were four huge ramparts to protect the hilltop settlement.

Excavations in the 1930s by Dr (later Sir) Mortimer Wheeler and by English Heritage archaeologists in the 1980s showed a pattern of roads and numbers of buildings and storage pits inside this enormous hillfort. By the time of the Roman conquest in AD 43 the site was thinly occupied but one of graves in a small cemetery near the eastern entrance contained the body of a man shot in the back by a bolt from a Roman ballista (an artillery weapon). Perhaps he had been defending the site or one of its neighbouring settlements against the advancing Roman army (see page 21).

Maiden Castle from the air with artist's impressions of the settlement and the inside of one of the round houses.

In the last few centuries BC, the climate was rather like that of today. The pattern of settlement and economy in Britain can be seen as three distinct regional traditions.

WESTERN BRITAIN

In the west of England, Wales, and northern Scotland, settlements were mostly defended farmsteads and small hamlets of various sorts. These include cliff castles in Cornwall and Wales, courtyard houses in Cornwall, enclosed farmsteads in north-west England, and duns and brochs in Scotland. Small field systems and grazing plots often lay around the settlements. The economy relied heavily on livestock grazed on open ground, with crops cultivated in the small garden-sized plots near to the settlements. These farmers may have driven their flocks to higher ground in summer months.

CENTRAL ENGLAND

In southern central England, the Welsh Marches, parts of the Pennines and the Scottish borders, various types of settlement can be identified. Many of the early hillforts fell out of use about 400 BC, but a few were rebuilt as much larger and more elaborate defended enclosures. Danebury, Hampshire, is one of the best known examples. Such hillforts often occur at intervals of about 25-30 km, and it has been suggested that they were the centres of emerging political units, each with a petty king or chief at the head. It is possible that these leaders lived in the main hillfort together with their close supporters, craftspeople, priests and others of rank. Available evidence also suggests that the hillforts were community storage facilities for grain and livestock, a trading centre, a secure area to retreat to in troubled times and perhaps a ritual or religious place, with the leaders living close by.

Other settlements

Around the larger hillforts there were numerous smaller settlements represented by enclosures of different sorts and in some cases groups of houses on their own. These were the farms and homes of the majority of the population.

EASTERN AND SOUTH EASTERN ENGLAND

In the Midlands, eastern England and East Anglia hillforts were rare and here settlements included village-like groups of houses, and enclosures representing farmsteads and hamlets. The landscape was well ordered with fields defined by hedges and ditches, trackways linking settlements, and unenclosed grazing areas beyond the more intensively enclosed farmland.

LIVING ON THE EDGE OF THE EMPIRE

The pattern of regional variety in settlement described above remained roughly constant until the Roman Conquest but alliances between neighbouring groups probably developed. One reason for this may be that from about 50 BC the Roman Empire had expanded into Gaul (France and some adjoining countries) and from this time onwards southern Britain at least was living in the shadow of what at the time was one of the world's super-powers. This is the first period in Britain's past for which documentary evidence exists. We have, from Roman sources, the names of tribes and some individuals, for example.

ROMAN INFLUENCE

Southern and south-eastern England was most affected by the neighbouring Roman Empire. Here, some communities were strongly influenced by the affluence and high-living of the Roman world, and tried to copy Mediterranean customs by trading their goods for fine eating and drinking equipment, wine, luxury food, and exotic goods. Coins came into use, again following Mediterranean practices, and large settlements known as oppida (Colchester in Essex, for example)provided centres for trade and commerce in the years leading up to the Roman conquest. The wealthiest members of society were buried with provisions for an after-life - especially wine and luxury food. One particularly good example was excavated, and the barrow still survives at Lexden in Colchester.

The luxuries of the Roman world did not come cheap. Communities in the south east were trading in such commodities as silver, iron, grain, hunting dogs, and slaves, all of which were in great demand within the Roman empire. Little if any of this was available in south-eastern England, and must therefore have been obtained either by trade or less peaceful means from communities further north and west.

Except for those captured and sold as slaves, there was rather less direct contact with the Roman world, outside the south east of England, although occasional fragments of amphorae (wine, oil or sauce pottery containers) and other imported pottery suggest that some luxuries were occasionally enjoyed.

Life outside Roman influence

Most of the hillforts ceased to function in their traditional ways after about 50 BC, although people were still living inside some of them. Most of the population lived in their farmsteads and enclosed settlements. In the far west, the traditional pattern of small defended farmsteads and fortified enclosures continued as before.

Craftsmanship seems to have been a strong tradition among communities in the west, and in the last few decades before the Roman conquest, produced some of finest metalwork yet seen.

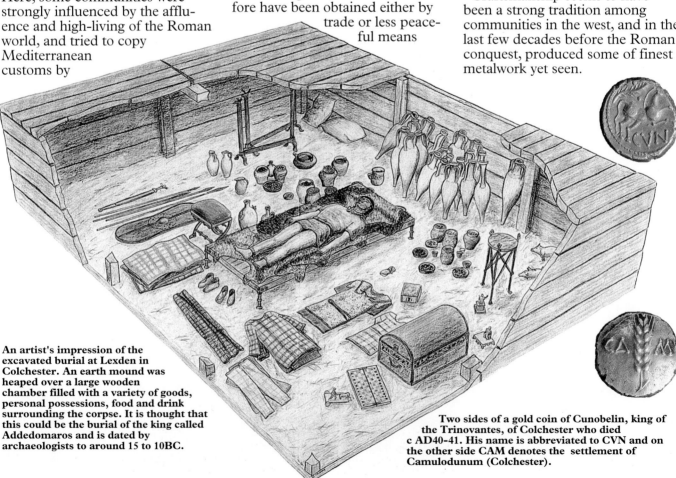

An artist's impression of the excavated burial at Lexden in Colchester. An earth mound was heaped over a large wooden chamber filled with a variety of goods, personal possessions, food and drink surrounding the corpse. It is thought that this could be the burial of the king called Addedomaros and is dated by archaeologists to around 15 to 10BC.

Two sides of a gold coin of Cunobelin, king of the Trinovantes, of Colchester who died c AD40-41. His name is abbreviated to CVN and on the other side CAM denotes the settlement of Camulodunum (Colchester).

THE FIRST ROMAN INVASIONS

According to his own accounts, Julius Caesar, later to be Emperor, visited Britain in 55 and 54 BC. Caesar had with him substantial military forces, but conquest does not seem to have been on his mind. More likely the visits were to develop trading links and to form alliances in order to secure stability along the northern boundary of the Empire.

In the years between Caesar's visits to Britain and the invasion of the Roman Emperor Claudius in AD 43 the political situation in Britain changed several times. For a while, the two largest tribes in southern England, the *Trinovantes* and the *Catuvellauni*, joined together. But this was relatively short-lived, and the general picture was one of increasingly strong chiefdoms which were competing with each other for supremacy and control over international trade. It was this slightly turbulent and always unpredictable situation that may have prompted Claudius to consider invading Britain.

THE FINAL INVASION

In AD 43 a Roman invasion force landed on the south coast. Quite why the Roman Empire invaded Britain at this time is not certain: political expediency by the Emperor Claudius is possible, as too the desire for access to the resources - especially the abundant grain harvest - already known to exist in Britain. Showing Roman support for alliances made with some of the tribal groups in the south east may also have played a role.

The conquest of Britain and its annexation to the Roman Empire was neither swift nor painless. Although some tribal groups immediately surrendered, in western and northern areas there was considerable resistance and period-ic revolt. The Romans had to fight their way across England taking settlement after settlement. It took four years to establish a frontier along what later became the Fosse Way from Exeter to Lincoln. Overall it took 30 years to subjugate what is now England and Wales. Scotland was never fully conquered and the same probably applies to the extreme southwest of England and much of Wales, although the borders here are less clearly marked.

Although the Romans imposed a new administrative structure, established towns, built a new road system, introduced new industries, and brought some of the trappings of life in heart of the Empire, there was little visible effect on local populations over most of the country until well into the second century AD. The basis of all modern British society had been laid many hundreds and thousands of years before the Romans arrived.

Chysauster

There are a number of stone-walled settlements in West Penwith, Cornwall, that were inhabited in the period immediately before and during the Roman occupation. The settlement at Chysauster, which can be visited, seems to have been built in the Roman period but inhabited for only about 100 years. Stone-walled settlements, like the one at Chysauster have three things in common:

■ they are made up of houses which have entrances onto a courtyard

■ most are within sight of a hillfort

■ most contain an associated *fogou* (a Cornish word meaning cave) used for underground cold storage, a place of safety or as a ritual building.

Although little material remains survive here because of the soil conditions, archaeological fieldwork has revealed an extensive system of fields around the settlement for growing cereal crops. It is also likely that the inhabitants of Chysauster kept horses, cattle, pigs and goats. It is also probable that the villages worked the local river for tin as a source of extra income or for barter.

ABOVE: An artist's impression of the village at Chysauster.

LEFT: The remains of the village today.

DOCUMENTARY EVIDENCE

By definition prehistoric sites have no contemporary documentary sources to tell us what went on. However, most prehistoric sites do have more recent documentary sources that you could use with your pupils to discuss topics such as:

■ how people in recent centuries and today have described a particular prehistoric site

■ what antiquarians, archaeologists or visitors thought a prehistoric site might have been used for - in other words, how it was interpreted

■ what issues have arisen over the preservation or presentation of an archaeological site.

Here are some examples of documentary sources for those three categories. Some extracts of documents have been translated from the Latin or had the spelling modernised.

Descriptions

'Staneges, where stones of wonderful size have been erected after the manner of doorways, so that doorway appears to have been raised upon doorway; and no one can conceive how such great stones have been so raised aloft, or why they were built there.'

1130 Henry of Huntingdon. This is the earliest documentary mention of Stonehenge describing, incorrectly, a monument with two stories of stones.

'The wind played, playing upon the edifice, produced a booming tune, like the note of some gigantic one-stringed harp.....The eastward pillars and their architraves stood up blackly against the light, and the great flame-shaped Sun-stone beyond them; and the Stone of Sacrifice midway.'

1889 Thomas Hardy. This is part of *Tess of the d'Urbervilles* describing the last moments of freedom of Tess at Stonehenge.

STONEHENGE, or GIANTS' DANCE, SALISBURY PLAIN. A Legend states :—'Aurelius, wishing to commemorate a battle, sent for Merlin, the Prophet, to consult on the proper monument to be erected to the memory of the slain ; he replied : "If you want an everlasting monument, send for the Giants Dance in Killarus, Ireland. There are stones of a vast magnitude, and wonderful quality." The Britons despatched 15,000 soldiers under Uther Pendragon. The removal was violently opposed by Gillomanus, a youth of wonderful valour, who exclaimed : "To Arms, Soldiers! While I have breath they shall not move one stone." A battle was fought and won by the Britons. Merlin then directed with a mystical and wonderful facility their removal When accomplished, Aurelius summoned the Clergy and the people to the Mount Ambrius, and a great solemnity was held for three days in honour of the event. Aurelius at his death was buried in the midst.

Although this postcard was sent in 1925 it still quotes the legendary origins of Stonehenge.

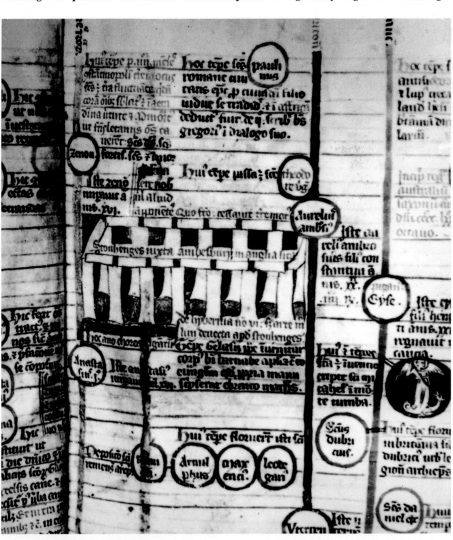

One of the earliest illustrations of Stonehenge from a fourteenth-century history of the world.

Interpretations

'Stonehenge was a monument erected in the reign of Aurelius Ambrosius by Merlin to perpetuate the treachery of Hengist, the Saxon general.'

'Send for the Giant's Round (says Merlin) which is on Mount Killarus in Ireland. In that place there is a stone construction which no man of this period could ever erect, unless he combined great skill and artistry....If they are placed in position round this site, in the way they are put up over there, they will stand for ever....'

1136 Geoffrey of Monmouth. Stonehenge was woven into the myths and legends about King Arthur. The idea that only gods or giants or wizards could have built such a monument, and not the 'primitive' peoples of prehistory, persisted until relatively recent times.

'Here Selbury, a round hill, riseth to a considerable height, and seemeth by the fashion of it, and by the sliding down of the earth about it, to be cast up by men's hands. Of this sort are many to be seen in this County, round and copped, which are call'd Burrows or Barrows, perhaps raised in memory of the Soldiers there slain. For bones are found in them; and I have read that it was the custom among the Northern People, that every soldier escaping alive out of Battel, was to bring his Helmet full of earth toward the raising of Monuments for their slain Fellows.'

1586 William Camden describing Silbury Hill in his book Britannia. See page 12 for a photograph of Silbury Hill.

Issues

'The real antiquary will always respect the Skeletons, Ashes, and Bones of the dead, which he may discover in his subterranean excavations. With hallowed feelings sanctified by the knowledge that dry bones shall live, he will do unto them as he would wish should be done unto his own remains. The Ashes and the Bones of the dead he will collect together with reverential awe, and he will never fail to restore those circling mounds of earth over them, which pointed out to him as they will point out to future Antiquaries, if not destroyed, the Tumuli of the Ancient Britons.'

1839 The Revd Charles Wools in his notes to his play *The Barrow Diggers.*

'Though the huts are still pretty entire, they are not so perfect as they were in 1849, many of the larger stones having been carried away for modern buildings, and it is to be regretted that similar acts of destruction have been recklessly practised, to the serious injury of other antiquities in the county.'

1861 J T Blight writing about Chysauster Ancient Village, Cornwall in *The Archaeological Journal.* See page 21 for a photograph of Chysauster.

'We come to Stonehenge because in an unstable world it is proper that the people should look for stability to the past in order to learn for the future....Holy land is holy and our right to be upon it cannot be denied.'

1978 From a letter to *The Times* from Sid Rawles who was the unofficial spokesperson for the unofficial free Stonehenge pop festivals.

Warrior queen of the Iceni

When prehistory touches history it is sometimes possible to use contemporary descriptions. There are a number of good descriptions of the pre-Roman peoples by Roman writers with some, like Julius Caesar, actually describing what they saw themselves. The first Roman invader of Britain describes the methods of chariot warfare his troops encountered:

'All the Britons paint themselves with a blue guide called woad. This gives them a more frightening appearance in battle. They wear their hair long and the men have moustaches.'

'This is their method of fighting from chariots: first, they dash about all over the battlefield hurling their javelins. Usually the enemy is terrified by the horses and the rumble of the chariot wheels. Then, the warriors leap down from their chariots and fight on foot while their drivers take the chariots to the edge of the battlefield to wait for a signal to collect them. Once back in the chariots these warriors are so skilled that they can run along the chariot pole between the horses, balance on the yoke and get back into the chariot as fast as lightning.'
Julius Caesar from *The War in Gaul.*

Boudica led her people, the Iceni, in an armed uprising of about 100,000 against the harsh Roman rule in Britain in AD60. Although the chariot is solidly sculpted here, we know from archaeological evidence that it would have been lightly built of wood and wickerwork and had no scythes

This statue at the end of Westminster Bridge opposite the Houses of Parliament is by the sculptor Thomas Thornycroft and was unveiled in 1902. It shows the famous warrior queen, Boudica.

on the wheels. Queen Boudica (or as she is incorrectly inscribed here Boadicea) strikes a classical pose but the classical writer Cassius Dio describes here as:

'This Bouduica, whom the Britons considered a worthy commander-in chief, was a very big woman, terrifying to look at, with a fierce look on her face. She had a harsh voice and wore her great mass of hair the colour of a lion's mane right down to her hips. She always wore a richly coloured tunic, a thick cloak fastened with a brooch and a large necklace of twisted gold around her neck. She used to brandish her spear to strike terror in the hearts of her warriors as she addressed them.'

EDUCATIONAL APPROACHES

Prehistory literally means 'before history' or, in other words, describes the period before writing was invented. The only evidence about the people and places of prehistory is the material remains left behind - for example, pieces of stone, bone or metal tools, fragments of pottery, or the evidence of settlements, rituals or burials they left in the landscape.

Archaeologists use a variety of methods to discover, uncover, record, analyse and interpret this evidence from prehistory. In many ways, archaeologists are like police detectives trying to solve a crime or journalists putting together a story by collecting various forms of evidence.

PREHISTORY AND INTERPRETATION

Once archaeologists have collected the evidence they attempt to interpret it. But archaeologists only ever find a tiny fraction of what was originally there. For instance, most organic evidence does not survive unless under very particular circumstances - for example, where the ground has remained waterlogged or frozen. Given such limitations, archaeologists use a range of scientific techniques to ask a number of standard questions including:

■ where were the objects made? - to see how far they had travelled before being excavated to provide information on social organisation and trade and exchange

■ how, and with what, were the objects made? - to study the level of technology available to the society

■ what animals were kept and what (if any) crops were grown - to understand what people ate and how they collected or produced their food.

However, even when these and other questions have been answered archaeologists still have

to interpret their results to provide an understanding of what life may have been like at a particular time in the past.

Objective interpretation?

Interpretation in prehistory is frequently compared to completing a complex jigsaw puzzle: prehistorians try to piece together the past fitting every element of the jigsaw into its correct place until a full picture is revealed. If this analogy is developed, interpretation in prehistory can be compared to trying to complete a jigsaw for which there is no picture on the box and for which 70% or more of the pieces have been lost. Given this scarcity of information, it is quite possible for two different archaeologists to come up with significantly different interpretations of the same set of physical remains. The basics may well be known, for example:

■ this group had developed the use of metals for tools, that group had not

■ this group lived mainly by gathering and hunting wild resources, that group lived mainly by cultivating domesticated crops.

However, once these basics have been ascertained, and it is not always easy to do this, there are all sorts of difficulties associated with more complex interpretation. Archaeologists may know, for example, that the society under discussion had flint tools, but have no information as to how such tools were used. They may know that houses were round or rectangular, but have little or no information as to whether there were upper floors, whether the walls were decorated or embellished with woven hangings or whether the structural posts were intricately carved and painted or if they were left as un-worked tree trunks. They may know that people would have needed some form of clothing, but have no information as to whether most was made from leather or whether most was woven, or whether it was dyed and patterned or rough and simple.

An artist's impression of the Bronze Age settlement at Grimspound, Devon. There are the remains of 24 houses in a walled enclosure of about 1.6ha (4 acres). You could use this drawing to ask pupils what evidence an archaeologist might have to find to commission the artist, for example: How do we know there were 24 houses - or that they were round? What sort of evidence would point to houses rather than storage places? What evidence would you need to suggest that the people at Grimspound kept cattle and sheep?

Only half the story?

The photograph (right) shows how English Heritage tried to encourage visitors to the museum at Avebury Stone Circle to think about the evidence and how it might be interpreted. The museum exhibition and displays tell the story of the circle, something about life at the time and how the circle was excavated in the 1920s and 1930s. This full-size Neolithic figure was deliberately dressed in two halves:

■ the half on the right shows a rather raggedly-dressed man coping with his existence. The clothes are dull and are based on one reading of the evidence.

■ the other half on the left shows a much more colourful figure. His body is painted and tattooed and his clothes are better made and has

different types of jewellery attached.

The two halves represent the extremes of interpretation in two respects. First, they represent some people's view that prehistoric people lived dull, rather barbaric lives while others that prehistoric people at this time were generally quite sophisticated - or they would not have been able to create a society which produced amazing monuments such as Avebury and Stonehenge.

Second, the 'dull' half is based purely on surviving evidence from fragments of fabric from graves, while the 'colourful' half used evidence from elsewhere in Britain (and Europe) where tattooed skin and beautifully-made jewellery has survived.

Part of the museum display at Avebury Wiltshire.

Classroom interpretation activities

Prehistory is an excellent educational tool for developing an enquiring and analytical mind. You could present your pupils with the challenge of interpreting evidence for themselves by playing the Dustbin Game.

Here is a photograph of a 'slice through' a real dustbin. You could easily produce similar evidence by tipping out the classroom's waste paper basket after a day's use. There are two routes you can guide your class along:

Route 1

What does this rubbish tell us about the people who threw it away?

Ask your class to point out the evidence to answer questions such as:

■ Are there any children in this family?

■ What kinds of food do they eat?

■ What sorts of pets do they have and how many?

■ What season of year is it? (The dustbin might have Easter egg wrappers or bits of Christmas decorations.)

Route 2

In the past, people got rid of their rubbish wherever they could - they dug pits, threw it into ditches, filled hollows in the landscape, used old wells and spread it on fields. Let's imagine that this dustbin-full has been buried somewhere. After some time quite a lot of it will have rotted away. Organic material (that is, things which were once living such as paper or wood) will tend to rot quicker than inorganic things (that is, things which were never 'alive' such as plastic and metal).

Ask your pupils to work out what the archaeologist might be left with after all the organic materials had rotted away. How difficult it might be, then, to reach conclusions about the people who threw this rubbish away?

Interpreting prehistory at this level becomes increasingly subjective and open to personal whim. In other words we can often know quite a lot about the non-social context of prehistory - the technology available to a particular group for example - but almost nothing about its social context - how the group was organised, what they looked like, and perhaps most intriguingly, what they thought about, what they believed, how they viewed the world.

We will never know with any real degree of certainty what the past was really like or what people really believed. Archaeologists create images of the past that are based on scientific understanding but they are only interpretations of what life may have been like and are open to constant review and re-interpretation. Archaeologists, together with artists or model-makers, often create pictures of a particular scene they have excavated, drawing on a variety of different forms of evidence. You will find a variety of artists' impressions of the past in this book, drawn and painted in different styles.

TECHNOLOGY AND PREHISTORY

Prehistory offers a wide range of opportunities for work in technology. Investigating and *doing* some of the tasks carried out in prehistory is one way of showing your pupils that people in the distant past were not 'stupid cave dwellers' or lived with the dinosaurs like Fred Flintstone.

Moving a brick henge

We do not know, absolutely, how or by what route the Sarsen stones (each weighing between four and 50 tonnes) were actually transported to Stonehenge. The smaller bluestones were probably moved as much as possible by water to make their transportation easier (see page 13). On land, both sets of stones would have had to be pulled, probably on sledges or rollers (tree trunks), by teams of people or, more likely, oxen harnessed to the stones with robes of leather or plant fibre.

However they were moved, the operation was an enormous feat of engineering and organization. Even

A crane was used to lift stones in the 1950s. The wooden decking was laid to protect the fragile archaeology below the ground.

For this experiment you will need

about 40 house bricks
parcel string
pencils or pieces of dowel to use as rollers
a variety of surfaces at least 1 metre long
spring balances.

if animal power was used it has been estimated that the whole task of building just the final phase of Stonehenge took 1.5 million work hours.

Moving the stones

Divide the pupils into groups and ask them to record what they did, write up their results and report back to the class. Ask each group to:

■ weigh one brick and measure its height, width and length

■ attempt to push the brick on a smooth, flat surface using only one finger tip to move it

■ record how many fingers were needed before the brick moved

■ try the same experiment on different surfaces, recording how many fingers (=effort) was needed for each surface.

Now give each group some string and suggest they try pulling the

Many visitors to Stonehenge, like these nineteenth-century gentlemen, have wondered how the huge stone were put up without the use of modern machinery. When the stone circles were excavated and consolidated in the early part of this century and again in the 1950s, no attempt was made to move the stones using 'prehistoric' technology, as you can see.

brick across the different surfaces and record:

■ what happens when each surface is lifted or lowered to various gradients

■ how much pulling power is needed by using the spring balance.

Next, give the groups some wooden rollers and ask them to:

■ experiment by using different numbers of rollers

■ record the difference made to the amount of effort required

■ find out the difficulties of moving the brick downhill.

How was it constructed?

Even today some feel that prehistoric people were not as 'clever' as we are today. Yet prehistoric sites and objects which survive today tell quite another story. Prehistoric people knew how to 'exploit' the resources in their environment much better than westernised people do today. They were skilled at measuring out and constructing complex buildings.

Visiting prehistoric sites is an opportunity to investigate structures which are often completely different from the sorts of buildings constructed in Roman, medieval and modern times. Yet prehistoric sites were constructed without the use of machinery. You might like to use a simple contrast to begin exploring that point.

There are many examples of huge earthwork projects in prehistoric times. Just look at the massive banks and ditches of Maiden Castle (see page 19) or the enormous mound of Silbury Hill (see page 12).

Where can you see earthwork construction today? On a small scale it is obvious on any building site, where the construction workers use digging machines to cut trenches for foundations and services. But massive earthmoving is carried out on all motorway construction with relatively few workers. Look for examples from the present and the past and ask your pupils to think about or research information, for example: (see below right)

RIGHT: An artist's impression of the building of the final phase of Stonehenge.

Consolidation of the stones during work in 1919-1926.

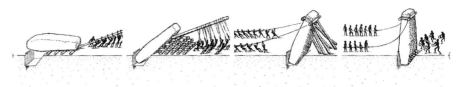

Excavation and careful recording of the stones has shown how the sarsen stones might have been erected in position using levers and wooden scaffolding, as the diagrams here explain.

TIME	PROJECT	SKILLS	RESOURCES
The present	Motorway	Accurate surveying	Heavy machinery
		Careful machine handling	Access to materials such as gravel and tarmac
Victorian times	Railway	Accurate surveying	Large workforce of 'navvies'
		Skilled workforce	Pickaxes, shovels & wheelbarrows
Medieval times	Castle	Accurate surveying	Large number of workers
		Skilled workforce	Pickaxes, shovels & baskets
			Large amounts of timber and stone
Prehistoric times	Settlement defences	Accurate surveying	Majority of the community
		Skilled workforce	Picks, shovels & baskets
			Axes for timber

27

Making fire

Until quite recently fire provided heat light, protection and cooked food for people in western societies. Most young children have no direct experience of making and using fire today. You could begin an activity on fire by discussing

■ where fire is still used today (for example, in smelting metals)

■ what has replaced fire as a means of cooking, lighting and heating in modern houses

and go on to look at, say, Victorian houses to investigate how fire was used and the materials needed to maintain fire.

You might then go on to create fire itself using the fire bow method described below.

Prehistoric nettle puree

Put the young nettle tops into boiling water and boil until tender. Drain well and chop finely. Reheat, adding butter and salt to taste.

Sorrel, dandelion, spinach, sow thistle, watercress and lady's smock may all be mixed for this puree (if the more bitter herbs of dandelion and sow thistle are used alone, change the water after 5 minutes boiling). Cooking in a liberal amount of fast-boiling water will conserve the vitamins better than slow, gentle cooking.

From *Food and cooking in prehistoric Britain*, see Bibliography.

Making fire and experimenting with prehistoric cooking.

To make fire a stick has to be rotated in another piece of wood with sufficient speed and pressure to cause the dust generated by friction to heat up until it combusts. It is easy to generate sufficient heat and lack of success is usually caused by moisture or lack of air. Air must be available, via a groove cut in the hearth, directly at the point of maximum friction.

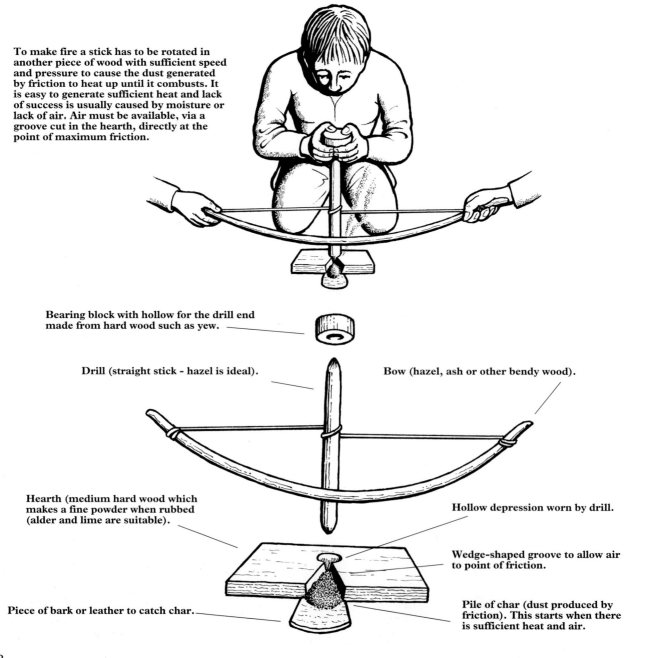

Bearing block with hollow for the drill end made from hard wood such as yew.

Drill (straight stick - hazel is ideal).

Bow (hazel, ash or other bendy wood).

Hearth (medium hard wood which makes a fine powder when rubbed (alder and lime are suitable).

Hollow depression worn by drill.

Wedge-shaped groove to allow air to point of friction.

Piece of bark or leather to catch char.

Pile of char (dust produced by friction). This starts when there is sufficient heat and air.

INTRODUCING LANGUAGE WORK

A useful on-site activity which provides excellent material for creative work back in the classroom is to ask pupils to find, draw or photograph particular areas of the site which conjure up particular feelings or moods. Ask pupils to identify areas which suggest:

fear	sadness
loneliness	happiness
relaxation	domination
fatigue	power

They could support their choices by adding three descriptive words or three actions associated with an activity in that area.

You could modify this exercise for younger pupils by asking them to find areas which they think would be:

hot	cold
dark	light
smelly	smoky
damp	dirty

Seeing, hearing and feeling

It is much easier to get pupils to write if you help them build up a set of appropriate words first. It is important that your class knows why they are collecting their words. Do you want them to do:

■ descriptive writing for their own guidebook or the script for an audio guide?

■ creative writing for a piece of poetry or diary entry or a letter from one of the prehistoric inhabitants?

It will be much easier to complete this back in the classroom, when the value of the collected words will show. You could easily produce your own activity sheet for use on the site visit. Use a photograph, plan, aerial shot or artist's impression in the centre and mark on the places you want your pupils to work on. Ask pupils to locate each marked area, then enter into the box the words that best describe that place. You might want to specify the number of words you ask them to think of.

Some of the fifteen visible stones of Mitchell's Fold Bronze Age stone circle, Shropshire.

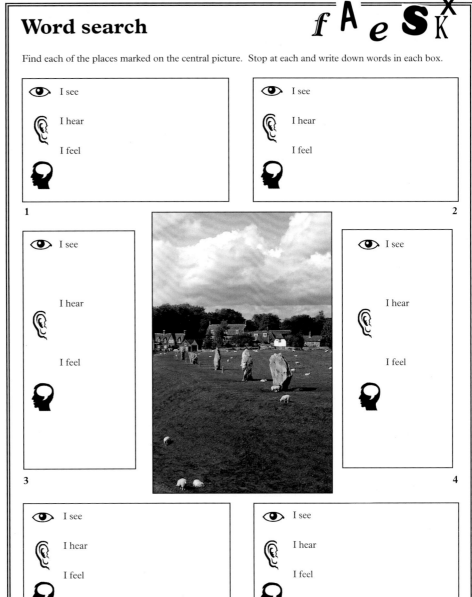

Word search

Find each of the places marked on the central picture. Stop at each and write down words in each box.

Boxes labelled 1–6, each containing:
- 👁 I see
- 👂 I hear
- I feel

If you want your class to imagine what the place was like when lived in or used in the past, you will need to give them some background information, but they can then think of words for themselves using the same I see, I hear, I feel list. For example, they might 'see' this stone circle reflected by moonlight, or 'hear' a mass of people coming across the hills for some ceremony there, or 'feel' the atmosphere change when they arrived inside the circle.

MATHS

Visits to prehistoric sites can provide opportunities for practising a variety of mathematical techniques, for example, at a stone circle or standing stone you might ask you pupils to:

■ measure by using standard or non-standard units of measurement

■ estimate height using a protractor and a scale drawing

■ calculate volume.

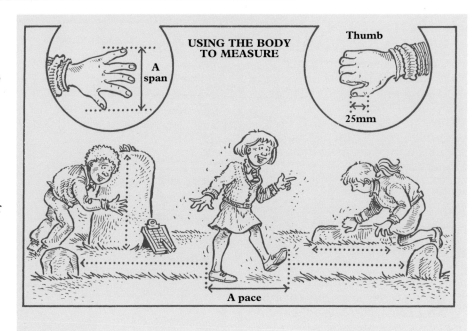

Volume

On prehistoric sites it is possible to work out the weight of individual standing stones using a simple method:

■ **Measure the width, height and depth of a stone.**

■ **Back at school use a piece of local stone, or preferably a piece of stone picked up near the site (but NOT from it, of course) to work out its volume by displacement (see drawing).**

Pupils on a visit to Avebury, Wiltshire.

■ **Work out the average volume of the prehistoric standing stone by calculating Height X Depth X Width.**

■ **Then divide the volume of the standing stone by the smaller sample:**

So the weight of the standing stone will be X multiplied by the weight of the sample stone.

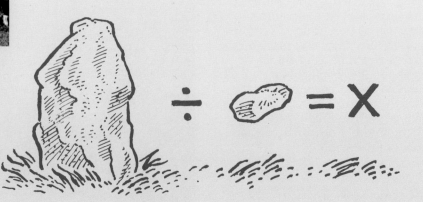

ISSUES

Prehistoric peoples created the British landscape we live in today. There have been many alterations since then and only a small proportion of what must have once been there has survived. There are a number of issues which you can discuss with your pupils including:

■ should we preserve as much as we can/everything/only a portion/nothing from our prehistoric past?

■ should modern development take precedence over past landscapes?

■ are the remains of the past an important part of our present and future society - if so should we spend more on them?

■ should ancient sites be freely open for people to visit, or will huge numbers of visitors destroy what we seek to protect?

■ should minority groups be allowed to 'claim' some prehistoric sites as their own?

Hundreds flocked to Stonehenge to watch the eclipse in 1999.

We do know that Stonehenge (see page 13) was constructed many centuries before Druids came to Britain. Indeed there is no evidence that the Druids had anything to do with Stonehenge at all. Their connection to this stone circle and others is largely due to the interpretation of these monuments by William Stukeley, an eighteenth-century antiquarian.

Will the barrow survive?

Many prehistoric burial mounds have survived on our landscape. However, many mounds and other ancient sites which are protected by law have been threatened by a variety of damaging activities, from burrowing rabbits to treasure hunters with metal detectors, from road widening schemes to antiquarian digging in the nineteenth century.

On the next page you will find a game which you can photocopy. While your pupils are playing this game, encourage them to think about and discuss the reasons for their gaining or losing points. Players will need dice and different coloured counters.

The body under the barrow

On page 33 you will find an activity sheet which you may photocopy for class use. Its aim is to investigate how much you can really discover about the person who was buried under Bush Barrow. You will find information about the barrow and an artist's impression of the burial ceremony on page 14. You could continue the activity in class by discussing how much more we might know about this prehistoric burial if the site had been excavated using modern scientific methods.

The bronze age barrow at Innisidgen, St Mary's on the Isles of Scilly.

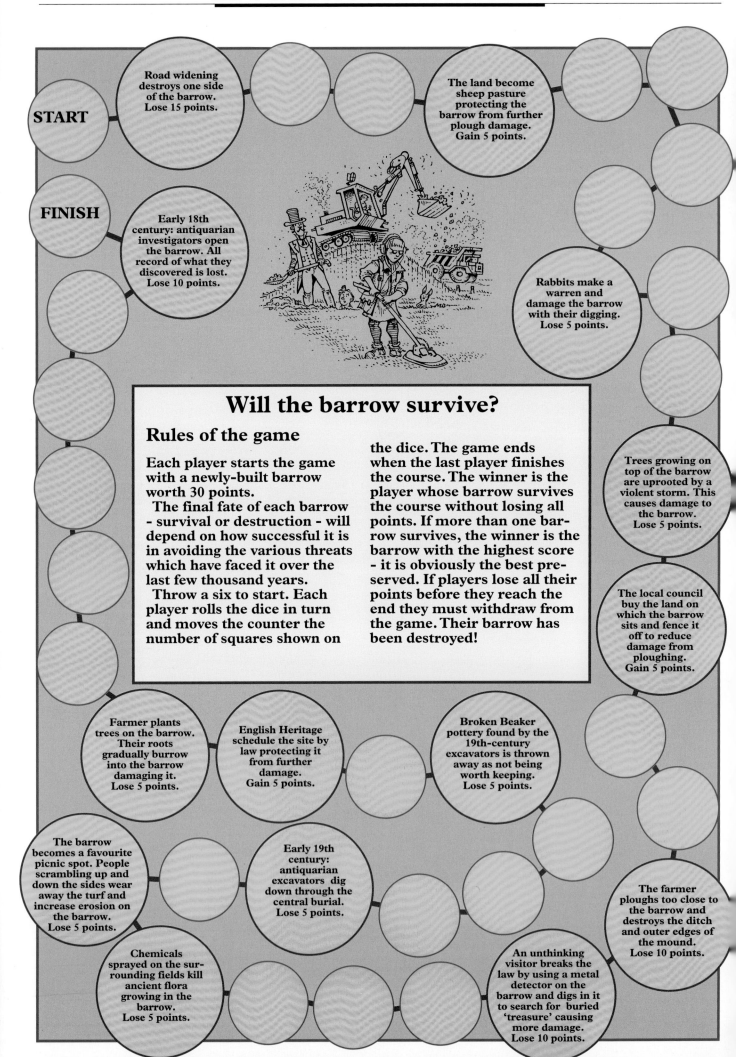

START

Road widening destroys one side of the barrow. Lose 15 points.

The land become sheep pasture protecting the barrow from further plough damage. Gain 5 points.

FINISH

Early 18th century: antiquarian investigators open the barrow. All record of what they discovered is lost. Lose 10 points.

Rabbits make a warren and damage the barrow with their digging. Lose 5 points.

Will the barrow survive?

Rules of the game

Each player starts the game with a newly-built barrow worth 30 points.

The final fate of each barrow - survival or destruction - will depend on how successful it is in avoiding the various threats which have faced it over the last few thousand years.

Throw a six to start. Each player rolls the dice in turn and moves the counter the number of squares shown on the dice. The game ends when the last player finishes the course. The winner is the player whose barrow survives the course without losing all points. If more than one barrow survives, the winner is the barrow with the highest score - it is obviously the best preserved. If players lose all their points before they reach the end they must withdraw from the game. Their barrow has been destroyed!

Trees growing on top of the barrow are uprooted by a violent storm. This causes damage to the barrow. Lose 5 points.

The local council buy the land on which the barrow sits and fence it off to reduce damage from ploughing. Gain 5 points.

Farmer plants trees on the barrow. Their roots gradually burrow into the barrow damaging it. Lose 5 points.

English Heritage schedule the site by law protecting it from further damage. Gain 5 points.

Broken Beaker pottery found by the 19th-century excavators is thrown away as not being worth keeping. Lose 5 points.

The barrow becomes a favourite picnic spot. People scrambling up and down the sides wear away the turf and increase erosion on the barrow. Lose 5 points.

Early 19th century: antiquarian excavators dig down through the central burial. Lose 5 points.

The farmer ploughs too close to the barrow and destroys the ditch and outer edges of the mound. Lose 10 points.

Chemicals sprayed on the surrounding fields kill ancient flora growing in the barrow. Lose 5 points.

An unthinking visitor breaks the law by using a metal detector on the barrow and digs in it to search for buried 'treasure' causing more damage. Lose 10 points.

THE BODY UNDER THE BARROW

In September 1808 the antiquarian Sir Richard Colt Hoare excavated Bush Barrow, near Stonehenge. He made no drawings of what he found, but did leave a written description of his discoveries. Read Sir Richard's description and try to fill in the answers to the questions.

1.
Do you think the body is male or female? Give evidence to support your answer.

2.
How did he/she die?

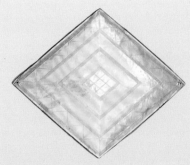

3.
Was the person rich or poor? How do you know?

'In reaching the floor of the barrow we discovered the skeleton lying south to north; the extreme length of the thigh bone was 20 inches. About 18 inches south of the head we found several brass rivets intermixed with wood...they were (probably) the moulded remains of a shield. Near the shoulders lay the fine celt (axe) ....originally furnished with a handle of wood. Near the right arm was a large dagger of brass, and a spearhead of the same metal. These were accompanied by a curious article of gold which had originally decorated the case of the dagger. The handle of wood belonging to this instrument exceeds anything we have yet seen...the decoration was formed by thousands of gold rivets, smaller than the smallest pin. So very minute were these pins that our labourers had thrown out thousands of them with their shovels before, by the necessary aid of a magnifying glass, we could discover what they were, but fortunately enough remained attached to the wood to develop the pattern. Beneath the fingers of the right hand lay a lance of brass, but so much corroded that it broke to pieces on moving. Immediately over the breast of the skeleton was a large plate of gold in the form of a lozenge, measuring 7 inches by 6 inches. It was perforated at the top and bottom for the purpose of probably fastening it to the dress as a breast plate. We next discovered, on the right side of the skeleton, a very curious perforated stone, some articles of bone, many small rings of the same material, and another article of gold. The stone had a wooden handle which was fixed into the perforation at the centre, and encircled by a neat ornament of brass, part of which still adheres to the stone.'
[1 inch = 2.5cm]

4.
Why do you think all these objects were buried with the body?

5.
What materials were used to make the objects buried with the body?

6.
Do you think all the objects were made by the same person? Give reasons for your answer.

WHAT HAPPENED TO PREHISTORIC PEOPLE?

There was, of course, no simple transition from prehistoric people (without their own written record) to people recorded by writings. We know something about the Celtic peoples from Roman and Greek writers. Perhaps some prehistoric peoples had writing but all the evidence has since been lost? Perhaps the 'writing' or at least the records do survive but we are not clever enough to read the symbols and signs today.

The Inuit people had a language but did not write it down. The Inuit called themselves 'Inuit' meaning 'the people' but neighbours called them Eskimo, meaning 'eaters of raw flesh'. When Europeans first visited them they started to write down what they heard, and so their language has been preserved. They were, nevertheless, 'prehistoric' people.

You might want your pupils to investigate 'prehistoric' peoples in other parts of the world. They will find plenty of evidence that today's 'prehistoric' peoples are not primitive or backward but as skilled, or more skilled, than many others in the world. Lifestyles based on hunting, fishing or gathering food can still be observed today in some parts of the world.

You will also find evidence for discussion about issues of how some western peoples treated those they 'discovered' in far off lands.

Endangered peoples

Many peoples today are still threatened with extinction, often because of the wholesale destruction of their environment. In the past it was usually because of invasion of westerners, their killing and their introduction of diseases to which the native population had no resistance. When the Portuguese arrived in Brazil, for example, in the sixteenth century there were about 1 to 2 million people who lived by hunting, fishing and gathering food. Only about 150,000 survive today.

Great Zimbabwe

There are a number of major monuments around the world for which no written record exists - the Easter Island Statues, for example. You might use examples like this to discuss how an interpretation of the monument might be reached using only the physical evidence and, perhaps, folk memory. How might an archaeologist travelling to a depopulated Earth in the future understand St Paul's Cathedral, or Wembley Stadium or the Millennium Dome, without the aid of documentary, visual or oral records?

The complex of stone buildings, walls and towers now called Great Zimbabwe, in Zimbabwe, was an ancient city dating from the twelfth century AD. As there were no surviving records its original name is unknown but in the Shona language the word 'zimbabwe' comes from either 'dzimba dza mabwe' ('houses of stone') or 'dzimba woye'('chief's houses'). By about AD 1350 we think that Great Zimbabwe was the residence of the most powerful ruler in south-eastern Africa and had a population of more than 10,000 people.

Most people farmed grain and bred cattle but the objects found during excavations revealed sculptors, jewellers, weavers and potters. The buildings and walls are well constructed so there must have been skilled construction designers and builders. Carved images of birds and animals have been found displayed which must indicate some ritual or religious beliefs.

It took great skill to built the dry stone walls at Great Zimbabwe. The top of the doorway here is made from a stone lintel.

Inside the Great Enclosure is this solid tower of stone, nearly ten metres high. It may have symbolised the power of the king who is thought to have lived nearby.

The Great Enclosure at Great Zimbabwe was built from a million blocks of granite stone. Inside the walls there were houses for five or six families, probably related to the king.

BIBLIOGRAPHY AND RESOURCES

Books for teachers

Barton, N, *Stone Age Britain*, Batsford/English Heritage, 1997. ISBN 0-7134-6846-7.

Bewley, R, *Prehistoric Settlements*, Batsford/English Heritage, 1994. ISBN 0-7134-6853-X.

Coles, J, *Experimental Archaeology*, Academic Press, 1979. ISBN 0-12-179752-X.

Cunliffe, B, *Danebury*, Batsford/English Heritage, 1993. ISBN 0-7134-6886-6.

Darvill, T, *Prehistoric Britain from the air*, Cambridge University Press, 1996. ISBN 0-521-55132-3.

Darvill, T, *Prehistoric Britain*, Routledge, 1996. ISBN 0-7134-51793.

Green, K, *Archaeology: An Introduction*, Routledge, 1996 ISBN 0-415- 16607-1. (An electronic companion is also available on Http:\\www.staff.ncl.ac.uk\kevin.greene\wintro\)

Malone, C, *Avebury*, Batsford/English Heritage, 1989. ISBN 0-7134-5960-3.

Molyneaux, B L, *Archaeological Themes: Prehistory*, NEAB/English Heritage/Council for British Archaeology, 1993. 0-901628-97-2.

Parker Pearson, M, *Bronze Age Britain*. Batsford/English Heritage, 1993. ISBN 0-7134-6856-4.

Pryor, F, *Flag Fen*, Batsford/English Heritage, 1991. ISBN 0-7134-6753-3.

Putnam, B, *The Prehistoric Age*, The Dovecote Press, 1998. ISBN 1-874336-62-8.

Renfrew, C, and Bahn, P, *Archaeology: Theories, Methods and Practice*, Thames & Hudson, 1996. ISBN 0-500-27605-6.

Reynolds, P J, *Farming in the Iron Age*, Cambridge University Press, 1976. ISBN 0-521-21-84-4.

Richards, J, *Stonehenge*, Batsford/English Heritage, 1992. ISBN 0-7134-6142-X.

Sharples, N, *Maiden Castle*, Batsford/English Heritage, 1991. ISBN 0-7134-6083-0.

Shire Publications on many aspects of archaeology, ethnography, rural history and country crafts. Each compact volume is written by an expert. Some relevant titles include:

Burl, A, *Prehistoric Stone Circles*, 1983, ISBN 0-85263-640-7.

Grinsell, L, *Barrows in England and Wales*, 1984, ISBN 0-85263-669-5.

Pollard, J, *Neolithic Britain*, 1997, ISBN 0-7478-0353-6.

Reid, M L. *Prehistoric Houses in Britain*, 1993, ISBN 0-7478-0218-1.

Reynolds, P, *Ancient Farming*, 1987, ISBN 0-85263-876-0.

Stuart, A, *Life in the Ice Age*, 1988, ISBN 0-85263-929-5.

A full list of titles is available from Shire Publications Ltd, Cromwell House, Church Street, Princes Risborough, Bucks HP27 9AJ.

Educational approaches

Anderson, C, Planel, P, and Stone, P, *A Teacher's Handbook to Stonehenge*, English Heritage, 1996, ISBN 1-85074-312-6.

Barnes, J, *Design and Technology and the Historic Environment*, English Heritage, 1999. ISBN 1-85074-399-1.

Collins, F & Hollinshead, E, *English and the Historic Environment*, English Heritage, 2000. ISBN 85074-330-4.

Copeland, T, *Geography and the Historic Environment*, English Heritage, 1993. ISBN 1-85074-332-0.

Copeland, T, *Maths and the Historic Environment*, English Heritage, 1992. ISBN 1-85074-329-0.

Corbishley, M (ed), *Primary History: Using the evidence of the historic environment*, English Heritage, 1999. ISBN 1-85074-650-8.

Coupland, L, *A Teacher's Handbook to the Avebury Monuments*, English Heritage, 1988, ISBN 1-85074-173-5.

Durbin, G, Morris, M, and Wilkinson, S, *Learning from Objects*, English Heritage, 1990. ISBN 1-85074-259-6.

Fairclough, J, *History through Role Play*, English Heritage, 1994. ISBN 1-85074-333-9.

Henson, D, *Teaching Archaeology: a United Kingdom Directory of Resources*, Council for British Archaeology/English Heritage, 1996. ISBN 1-872414-67-2.

Hill, J D, Mays, S, & Overy, C, *The Iron Age*, Archaeology and Education No. 9, University of Southampton, 1989. ISBN 0-85432-332-5.

Keen, J, *Ancient Technology*, English Heritage, 1996, ISBN 1-85074-448-3.

Lockey, M & Walmsley, D, *Art and the Historic Environment*, English Heritage, 1999. ISBN 1-85074-651-6.

Maddern, E, *Storytelling at Historic Sites*, English Heritage, 1992, ISBN 1-85074-378-9.

Planel, P, *The Boxgrove Excavations, Information for teachers*, English Heritage, 1995, Free publication available on request from English Heritage Education Service.

Pownell, J, and Hutson, N, *Science and the Historic Environment*, English Heritage, 1992. ISBN 1-85074-331-2.

Renfrew, J, *Food and cooking in Prehistoric Britain*, English Heritage, 1985, ISBN, 1-85074-533-1.

Stone, P, *The First Farmers*, Archaeology and Education No. 8. University of Southampton, 1990. ISBN 0-85432-366-X.

Wheatley, G, *World Heritage Sites*, English Heritage, 1996. ISBN 1-85074-446-7.

Videos

According to the Evidence, English Heritage, 1998. 30 minutes. Looking at sources of evidence for classroom discussion.

Archaeology at Work: Looking for and Uncovering the Past, English Heritage, 1994. 58 minutes. Looks at the methods used by archaeologists in fieldwork and excavation.

Archaeological Detectives, English Heritage, 1990/91. 79 minutes.

Ferriby Boats, English Heritage, 1994. 25 minutes. Uncovering bronze ages boats from the River Humber.

Flag Fen - prehistoric Fenland brought to life, English Heritage, 1993. 30 minutes.

Poster packs

Interpreting the Past, English Heritage, 1999. ISBN 1-85074-737-7. 6 A3 posters with 8pp teacher's notes.

Time Detectives, English Heritage, 2000. 6 A3 posters with 8pp teacher's notes.

BOOKS FOR PUPILS

Corbishley, M, *Britain before the Romans Activity Book*, British Museum Press, 1989. ISBN 0-7141-1387-5.

Corbishley, M, *Prehistoric Britain Activity Book*, British Museum Press, 1989. ISBN 0-7141-1394-8.

Corbishley, M, *The Celts Activity Book*, British Museum Press, 1989. ISBN 0-7141-1393-X.

Corbishley, M, *How do we know where people came from?* Simon and Schuster, 1993. 0-7500-1310-9.

Corbishley, M, *What do we know about prehistory?* Simon and Schuster, 1994, 0-7500-1324-9.

Cork, B, and Reid, S, *The Usborne Young Scientist*, Archaeology, Usborne, 1991. ISBN 0-86020-865-6.

Place, R, *Clues from the Past*, Wayland, 1993. ISBN 0-7502-0677-2.

Wilkinson, P, (ed) *Early People*, Dorling Kindersley, 1989. ISBN 0-86518-342-5.

Fiction for pupils

Burnham, J & Ray, T, *Children of the stones, Carousel*, 1977. ISBN 0-552-52067-5.

Christopher, J, *Dom and Va*, Hamish Hamilton, 1979. ISBN 0-241-02329-7.

Fidler, K, *The Boy with the Bronze Axe*, Penguin, 1968. ISBN 0-1403-0563-7.

Garner, A, *The Stone Book Quartet*, Harper Collins, 1992. ISBN 0-00-184289-7.

John, M, *Blue Stone*, Barn Owl Press, 1982. ISBN 0-907117-27-9.

Kurten, B, *Dance of the Tiger*, Abacus, 1982. ISBN 0-349-12121-4.

Sutcliff, R, *Warrior Scarlet*, Puffin, 1968. ISBN 0-14-030895-4.

Treece, H, *The Dream Time*, Heinemann, 1974. ISBN 0-435-12196-0.

Walsh, J P, *The Dawnstone*, Piccolo, 1973. ISBN 0-330-25735-8.

Williams, R, *People of the Black Mountains*, Paladin, 1990. ISBN 0-586-9058-4.

Woodbridge, R, *Sheldra a child in Neolithic Orkney*, Tempus Reparatum, 1988. ISBN 1-871314-003.

English Heritage Education has published free information sheets for all the sites in its care, including prehistoric sites (see address on page 36). Also free for teachers are 8-page booklets with information and learning opportunities for the following prehistoric sites: *Chysauster Ancient Village*, Cornwall *Long Barrows in Gloucestershire* (includes Belas Knap, Hetty Peglar's Tump, Notgrove, Nympsfield and Rodmarton).

Also freely available are *'Learning beyond the classroom: information for Newly Qualified Teachers'*, *'Using English Heritage sites during residential visits'* and *'Stonehenge: information for tutors and students of GNVQ Leisure and Tourism'*.

ACTIVITY CENTRES

The activity centres listed here usually have reconstructed buildings and have special facilities/programmes for educational groups. The list was supplied by the Council for British Archaeology who provide advice and resources for teachers. They can be contacted at Bowes Morrell House, 111 Walmgate, York YO1 9WA (WEB site www.britarch.ac.uk).

Ancient Technology Centre
Cranborne Middle School,
Cranborne, Dorset BH21 5RP
Tel: 01725 517618

Archaeolink
Oyne, near Insch, Aberdeenshire
Tel: 01464 851500

Brigantium
Rochester, Otterburn,
Northumberland NE19 1RH
Tel: 01830 520801

Butser Ancient Farm
Nexus House, Gravel Hill,
Horndean, Hampshire PO8 0QE
Tel: 01705 558500

Castell Henllys Iron Age Fort
Felindre Farchog, Newport,
Pembrokeshire SA41 3UT
Tel: 01239 891319

Cheddar Showcaves
Cheddar Gorge, Somerset
Tel: 01394 742343

Creswell Crags Visitor Centre
Crags Road, Welbeck, Worksop S80 3LH
Tel: 01909 720378

Cockley Cley Iceni Village
Estate Office, Cockley Cley,
Norfolk PE37 8AG
Tel: 01760 721339

Cornwall Celtic Village
Saveock Mill, Greenbottom, Truro TR4 8QQ
Tel: 01872 560351

Hinchingbrooke Country Park
Huntingdon
Tel: 01480 451568

Iron Age Activity Centre
Michelham Priory, Upper Dicker,
Hailsham, East Sussex BN27 3QS
Tel: 01323 844224

New Barn Field Centre
Bradford Peverel, Dorchester, Dorset
Tel: 01305 268865

Scottish Crannog Centre
Croft na Caber, Kenmore, Loch Tay, Perthshire PH15 2HW
Tel: 01887 830583

Trewortha Farm Centre
North Hill, 12 Men's Moor,
Launceston, Cornwall
Tel: 01872 572725

OPPOSITE: Early Bronze Age flint arrowhead from Irthlingborough, Northamptonshire.

English Heritage is the national leader in heritage education. We aim to help teachers at all levels to use the resource of the historic environment. Each year we welcome over half a million pupils students and teachers on free educational visits to over 400 historic sites in our care. For copies of our *Free Educational Visits* booklet, our *Resources* catalogue, and *Heritage Learning*, our free termly magazine, contact:

**English Heritage Education
Freeport 22 (WD214)
London W1E 7EZ
Tel. 020-7973 3442
Fax. 020-7973 3443
www.english-heritage.org.uk**